MW01251137

CORE CONTENT LIBRARY

ANIMAL
TOP
10

Animal Appetites

Joanne Mattern

RED
CHAIR
•PRESS•

Earth's Amazing Animals is produced and published by Red Chair Press:

Red Chair Press LLC   PO Box 333   South Egremont, MA 01258-0333

www.redchairpress.com

Publisher's Cataloging-in-Publication Data

Names: Mattern, Joanne, 1963–

Title: Animal top 10. Animal appetites / Joanne Mattern.

Other Titles: Animal top ten. Animal appetites | Animal appetites | Core content library.

Description: South Egremont, MA : Red Chair Press, [2019] | Series: Earth's amazing animals | Includes glossary, Power Word science term etymology, fact and trivia sidebars. | Interest age level: 007-010. | Includes bibliographical references and index. | Summary: "Which animal swallows its food whole and then doesn't eat again for weeks? And did you know one animal eats only one food all its life? But it eats a lot of that food!"--Provided by publisher.

Identifiers: LCCN: 2018955618 | ISBN 9781634406949 (library hardcover) | ISBN 9781634407908 (paperback) | ISBN 9781634407007 (ebook)

Subjects: LCSH: Animals--Food--Juvenile literature. | Animals--Juvenile literature. | CYAC: Animals--Food. | Animals.

Classification: LCC QL751.5 .M386 2019 (print) | LCC QL751.5 (ebook) | DDC 591.53--dc23

Copyright © 2020 Red Chair Press LLC

RED CHAIR PRESS, the RED CHAIR and associated logos are registered trademarks of Red Chair Press LLC.

All rights reserved. No part of this book may be reproduced, stored in an information or retrieval system, or transmitted in any form by any means, electronic, mechanical including photocopying, recording, or otherwise without the prior written permission from the Publisher. For permissions, contact info@redchairpress.com

Illustrations by Tim Haggerty.

Photo credits: cover, pp. 5, 6, 7, 10–15, 18, 22, 23, 25–28, 36 (top), 37 (bottom) 39 iStock; pp. 3, 16, 19, 21 (bottom), 24, 32, 35 Shutterstock; p. 9 © Michael Durham/Minden Pictures; p. 17 © Chien Lee/Minden Pictures; p. 21 (top) © F1online digitale Bildagentur GmbH/Alamy; p. 29 © WaterFrame/Alamy; pp. 30, 31 \© Francios Gohier/VWPics/Alamy; p. 33 (top) © Roland Seitre/Minden Pictures; p. 33 (bottom) © MYN/Paul van Hoof/Minden Pictures; p. 36 (bottom) © Thomas Marent/Minden Pictures; p. 37 (top) © Stephen Dalton/Minden Pictures.

Printed in United States of America

0519 1P CGF19

Table of Contents

Introduction

Are you hungry? Every creature needs food to live. But some eat a lot more than others! And what you think of as a big meal might be just a snack for some members of the animal world.

Just like people, animals need food to give them energy. Some animals eat a lot because they need a lot of energy to survive. Others eat a lot because they have trouble digesting their food. And some animals eat a huge meal and then won't eat again for days. Each animal has its own unique and sometimes unusual way for finding and eating its food.

We've put together a list of the Top Ten Animal Appetites. Take a look and see why these animals have the biggest appetites on Planet Earth!

And the Winners Are...

Here are our choices for the Top 10 Appetites. Turn the pages to find out more about each of these creatures' big appetites.

10. The Giant Panda

9. The Little Brown Bat

8. The Caterpillar

7. The Hummingbird

6. The Python

5. The Argentine Wide-mouthed Frog

4. The Tasmanian Devil

3. The Tiger Shark

2. The Blue Whale

1. The Pygmy Shrew

10 The Giant Panda

A giant panda eats pretty much one thing and one thing only. Bamboo is a giant panda's favorite—actually, its only—food. A giant panda will eat between 25 and 40 pounds (11–18 kg) of bamboo a day! Imagine 40 pounds of food on your dinner plate!

Oddly enough, the panda's body is not very good at digesting bamboo. To make matters worse, bamboo does not provide a lot of **nutrition**. So it takes a lot of bamboo to give the panda the nutrition it needs to survive.

The natural habitat of the giant panda in central China is disappearing as farming and development expand.

It's a Fact

A panda can spend up to 14 hours a day eating.

9 The Little Brown Bat

The little brown bat is a big eater! This flying **mammal**'s favorite food is insects. Little brown bats will eat moths, wasps, beetles, gnats, and mosquitoes. A bat can eat half its own body weight in insects every night. Because little brown bats eat so many mosquitoes, they are good friends to people.

These bats are great hunters. They can snatch insects right out of the air, or grab them off of tree branches or leaves. These little bats are fast flyers too. A little brown bat can zip along at more than 12 miles an hour (19 km/h).

This little bat's body is only 2.5 to 4 inches (6.5–10 cm) long.

It's a Fact

Bats use echolocation to find their prey. They make squeaking noises that bounce off objects—including insects—and back to the bat's ears.

8 The Caterpillar

From the day it is born, a caterpillar does just one thing. It eats and eats and eats some more. Caterpillars are **herbivores**. That means they only eat plants. Most caterpillars only eat leaves, but some do eat seeds or flowers too.

Some caterpillars only eat one kind of plant. That plant is called the host plant. A butterfly lays its eggs on the host plant. As soon as the eggs hatch, the caterpillars start to munch. It's nice to have food ready right away!

It's a Fact

A few kinds of caterpillars don't eat plants. They eat tiny, soft insects instead.

A caterpillar built this chrysalis hidden under a leaf.

Caterpillars change into butterflies or moths through **metamorphosis**. After a few weeks, a caterpillar will build a cocoon or chrysalis around its body. Hidden from sight, the caterpillar's body will change completely. In time, a butterfly or moth will come out. It takes a lot of energy for a caterpillar to change into a butterfly or moth. That's why the caterpillar has to eat so much.

Power Word: *Metamorphosis* is from ancient Greek meaning: changing (*meta*) shape (*morph*) process of (*osis*). The process of changing shape or form.

7 The Hummingbird

The hummingbird is the smallest bird in the world. Some species of this tiny flyer are just three inches long and weigh less than a nickel. The smallest hummingbird is the bee hummingbird. It is only about two inches long—about the size of a big bee.

Hummingbirds are always in motion. They fly, swoop, and dive. Their wings move so fast—about 50 to 200 flaps a second—that these birds can hover in the air like a helicopter.

It takes a lot of energy to move so fast all the time. To get that energy, hummingbirds need a lot of food. Hummingbirds sip **nectar** from flowers. This sweet liquid is almost pure sugar, so it gives the hummingbird a lot of energy. A hummingbird needs to eat half its weight in sugar every day. To do this, the bird flies from flower to flower, licking up nectar with its tongue.

Hummingbirds can fly up, down, forward, backward and side-to-side.

It's a Fact

A hummingbird's heart beats 1200 times a minute. A person's heart only beats 60–100 times per minute!

Hummingbirds have good eyesight. They look for brightly colored flowers to feed on. Many people put out hummingbird feeders filled with red liquid to attract these tiny, hungry birds.

6 The Python

Imagine swallowing an animal that is bigger than your head. A snake called the python does this all the time. A python is one of the largest snakes in the world. Some species can measure up to 30 feet (9 m) long. Others are smaller—about seven feet (2 m) long.

Pythons are **carnivores**. They will eat almost any animal. Favorite meals include lizards, monkeys, and antelope. Pythons that live near people will eat pigs and other farm animals.

Australian black-headed python mid-meal.

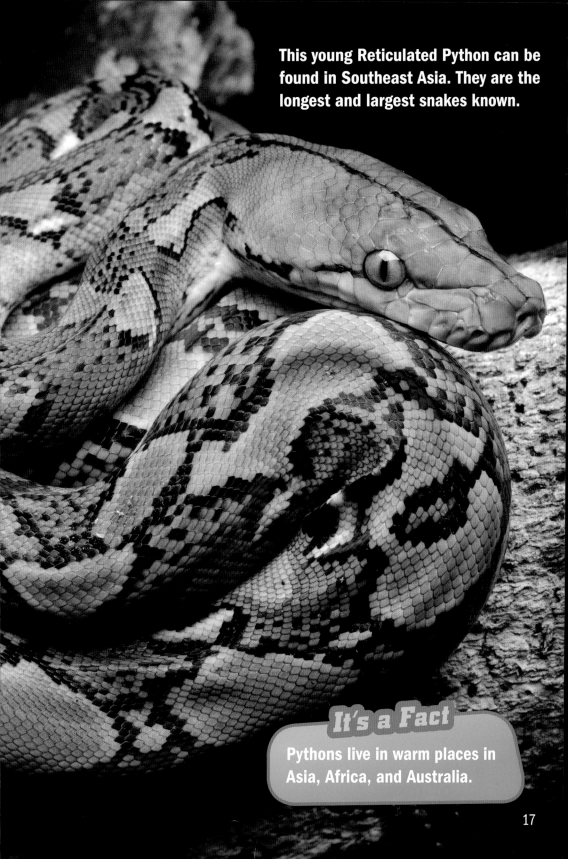

This young Reticulated Python can be found in Southeast Asia. They are the longest and largest snakes known.

It's a Fact

Pythons live in warm places in Asia, Africa, and Australia.

This python is constricting a deer.

A python kills its prey by **constriction**. A python grabs its prey with its teeth. Then it wraps its body around the animal and squeezes until the animal stops breathing. Once its prey is dead, the snake opens its mouth and slowly swallows the animal whole. The snake can do this because its jaw stretches very wide.

Once it has eaten, the python will find a quiet place to digest its food. It may not eat again for weeks or months.

5 The Argentine Wide-mouthed Frog

This frog has a big mouth! It's easy to see how the Argentine wide-mouthed frog got its name. A female measures about 6½ inches (16.5 cm) long. Males are about 4½ inches (11 cm) long. This frog's mouth is about half the size of the whole frog.

Argentine wide-mouthed frogs will try to eat anything that comes near their big mouths. This frog sits very still and waits for its prey to come close. Then it grabs the prey in its mouth. The frog's most common foods are insects, rodents, and other frogs. This frog will even try to eat animals that are bigger than the frog itself. Sometimes it even jumps toward its prey.

An Argentine frog's bite is very painful. The frog does not have teeth, but it does have sharp tooth-like bumps in its mouth. But since this frog is not venomous, its bite cannot kill a person or a large animal.

It's a Fact

This frog is sometimes called the Pacman frog, after the big-mouthed character in the video game.

Jumping for prey

Like their name suggests, Argentine wide-mouthed frogs live in Argentina. They also live in other parts of South America, including Brazil and Uruguay. These frogs live in grasslands, where there are lots of insects and rodents to eat.

4 The Tasmanian Devil

You may have seen the Tasmanian devil in cartoons. This crazy character is based on a real animal. And the real thing has a big, scary appetite!

Young Tasmanian devil

Tasmanian devils live in Australia. Like many Australian animals, Tasmanian devils are **marsupials**. They give birth to tiny babies that are not fully developed. After birth, the babies crawl into a pouch on the mother's body. They nurse on their mother's milk and stay in the pouch for about four months.

Tasmanian devils are not very big. They are just about two feet (0.6 m) long and weigh only 9 to 26 pounds (4–12 kg). But don't be fooled! This animal has a big appetite. It eats birds, snakes, fish, and insects. Tasmanian devils are also **scavengers** that eat dead animals.

Nothing goes to waste when this creature eats.

Nothing goes to waste when a Tasmanian devil has a meal. The devil eats every part of its prey's body, including fur, teeth, and bones. If a group of Tasmanian devils gathers to eat a dead animal, they will often fight each other for the best parts.

You would not want to be in a fight with a Tasmanian devil. This creature has very sharp teeth. When it fights, it hisses, growls, and snaps at its attacker. Tasmanian devils also howl and scream. This is one animal that is not good company at dinner!

The Tiger Shark

The great white shark has a bad reputation as a big eater. But the tiger shark has the biggest appetite in the shark family. These sharks will eat almost anything.

Young tiger sharks have tiger-like stripes on their body.

Tiger sharks live all over the world. They like warm water and are often found near islands, such as Hawaii or the Bahamas. They usually stay deep in the water during the day and come out at dusk or after dark to hunt.

Almost nothing is safe from a tiger shark. These sharks will eat turtles, birds, fish, seals, and other sharks. They also eat garbage they find in the water. Scientists have found all sorts of things in tiger shark stomachs, including nails, tires, and even car license plates! Being able to eat such a wide range of food helps the tiger shark survive. If an animal only eats one or two kinds of prey, it could starve if its prey disappears. But a tiger shark will always be able to find something to eat.

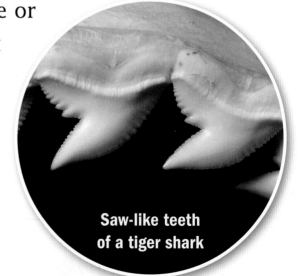

Saw-like teeth of a tiger shark

One reason a tiger shark can eat almost anything is the special way it chews its food. Most sharks have sharp teeth that can grab and hold prey. Tiger sharks have two rows of 24 teeth. These teeth are shaped to cut and saw. This allows them to crack turtle shells or chew up almost any kind of food—even metal or tires!

It's a Fact

Female tiger sharks only give birth every three years.

Tiger sharks are very large, between 10 and 14 feet in length and 850 to 1400 pounds in weight.

2 The Blue Whale

The blue whale is the largest animal in the world. In fact, it is the largest animal that ever lived! Even dinosaurs weren't this big. But here's something weird—this giant creature eats the tiniest food! The size of its prey means that it takes a lot of food to fill a blue whale's stomach.

A blue whale can be up to 100 feet (30.5 m) long. These giants weigh up to 160 tons. Even baby blue whales are huge. A newborn blue whale is about 23 feet (7 m) long and weighs 30 tons. A baby eats enough to gain 200 pounds (90 kg) a day!

The blue whale is a graceful swimmer but can reach speeds of over 30 km/hour.

Blue whales do not have teeth. Instead, they
have giant plates of **baleen** in their mouths.
A blue whale has hundreds of baleen plates in
its jaws. The whale sucks in water as it swims.
Then it pushes the water out of its mouth. The
baleen strains out any animals in the water for
the whale to eat.

It's a Fact

Baleen is made out of the
same material as a person's
nails and hair.

So what kind of food does a blue whale eat? It eats tiny **crustaceans** called krill. These crunchy creatures are only about two inches long. A blue whale can eat about 8,000 pounds (3.5 metric tons) of krill a day.

A blue whale's appetite is not the only big thing about it. This animal's heart is the size of a small car. That heart pumps ten tons of blood through its body.

An animal as big as a blue whale could never live on land. Its body would be too heavy to walk, and its lungs and other organs would be crushed by the animal's weight. But the ocean is the perfect home for this giant because the water helps support the animal's amazing weight.

The Pygmy Shrew

And now, we present the animal with the #1 appetite—THE PYGMY SHREW!

It's a Fact

Pygmy shrews only live about 18 months. They have the shortest life of any mammal.

The word "pygmy" means "small," and that's exactly what the pygmy shrew is. These tiny mammals weigh about as much as a penny and are only two inches (5 cm) long, including the tail. But these little creatures have an amazing appetite. They are hungry all day long, and they spend almost all their time hunting.

A pygmy shrew can eat its weight in food every day. That would be like a grizzly bear eating an elk every day, or a kid eating 15 pounds (7 kg) of food at every meal. But since a pygmy shrew is small, its prey is small too. These mammals eat insects, worms, spiders, and snails. The shrew grabs its prey with its sharp front teeth. Then it chews it with the flat, crushing teeth in the back of its mouth.

A pygmy shrew needs to eat so much because it needs a lot of energy. A resting shrew's heart beats up to 1,000 beats a minute, and it breathes about 800 times a minute. When it moves, a shrew's heart and lungs work even harder. To get enough energy to survive, a shrew has to eat almost all day long.

Shrews don't even get a break in the winter. They cannot build up enough body fat to hibernate, and if they stop eating, they will die. To stay warm in the winter, shrews stay underground, under the snow. They can find plenty of insects and worms to eat in the ground. Shrews also grow a thick coat of fur to keep them warm during the cold months.

In North America, the Pygmy shrew lives from Alaska to the east coast of Canada and south to parts of the Rocky and Appalachian mountains.

Hungriest Animals Runners-Up

Here are a few more creatures that didn't quite make the Top 10, but are still have pretty amazing appetites!

Elephant

Leech

Locust

Vulture

What's Your Top 10?

You've seen our list
of the Top 10 Hungriest
Animals and some runners-up
as well. Now it's your turn! Which
animals in this book do YOU think have the most amazing
appetites? Are there other animals that you think should
be on the list? Check your library or go on the Internet and
find photos and information on all that's appetizing in the
animal world. Then make your own Top 10 list!

Glossary

baleen a tough material in the mouths of some whales

carnivores animals that eat other animals

constriction squeezing

crustaceans animals that live in water and have a hard shell, such as shrimp or crabs

digesting breaking down food and changing it to energy

echolocation finding objects by bouncing sound waves off of them

herbivores animals that only eat plants

mammal a warm-blooded animal that has fur, gives birth to live young, and nurses its babies

marsupials mammals that give birth to undeveloped young and have a pouch

metamorphosis completely changing the body into an adult form

nectar a sweet liquid found inside some flowers

nutrition providing the food necessary to stay alive and grow

prey animals eaten by other animals for food

scavengers animals that eat dead animals

Learn More in the Library

Discover more interesting facts about our Top 10 Hungriest Animals. Search out facts about each of the animals on our list.

Bjorklund, Ruth. *Tasmanian Devils (Nature's Children).* Scholastic, 2013.

Jazynka, Kitson. *Mission: Panda Rescue.* National Geographic Children's Books, 2016.

Silverman, Buffy. *Tiger Sharks in Action.* Lerner, 2017.

Index

About the Author

Joanne Mattern is the author of nearly 350 books for children and teens. She began writing when she was a little girl and just never stopped! Joanne loves nonfiction because she enjoys bringing science topics to life and showing young readers that nonfiction is full of compelling stories! Joanne lives in the Hudson Valley of New York State with her husband, four children, and several pets!